Mentoring in Schools

The way to SUCCEED

Pam & John Richardson

ISBN 978-0-9571424-0-4

Mentoring in Schools

The way to SUCCEED

Pam & John Richardson

Contents

CHAPTER FIVE

CHAPTER SIX

ACKNOWLEDGEMENTS

We would like to thank James Moore and Rob McDougall for creating the opportunity to work with the Military 2 Mentor Programme. We have been truly inspired by Nikki Langston, Simon Poole, Everton Williams, Ricky Miller, Jon Colley, Gary Chapman, Tony Shuttleworth, Mick Walker and Paul Thompson. You are an amazing group of people and we are very grateful for all your input and feedback throughout the Military 2 Mentor programme.

Our thanks go to Michelle Crossland, Director of Intuition Discovery and Development Ltd for her vision and for her continued support and dedication in bringing this book into being.

Thanks also go to the staff at Lightning Source UK Ltd who have provided us with the answers to all our questions.

FOREWORD

The aim of this book, "Mentoring in Schools: The Way to Succeed" by Pam and John Richardson, is to provide an aide memoire for mentors of young people with a ready reference for safe and effective mentoring best practice. The book also supports the Institute of Leadership and Management accredited mentoring course provided by Intuition Discovery and Development Ltd on the Military to Mentor programme that is managed by SkillForce.

SkillForce is an education charity working with over 10,000 young people throughout 150 schools in Great Britain. Our instructors are mainly service leavers and educational sector specialists, who work in partnership with schools to deliver a curriculum and activities that provide young people with knowledge, skills, experience and long term personal support and most importantly, the self belief to aspire and achieve. Latterly, we have come to realise there was a specialist role within our organisation for the young person's mentor, someone who could take the SkillForce vision one stage further, and engage one to one with young persons, and by working closely with them and using life experiences and personal example, help and guide them to overcome obstacles to success.

When the Department for Education approached SkillForce to plan, design and deliver a Military to Mentors Programme with its partners, Endeavour and Knowsely Skills Academy in March 2011, we were well aware of the tremendous challenge and unique opportunity that presented itself. The aim of the programme, to select and train former members of the armed forces to become mentors to young people in schools across England, was in complete accord with SkillForce's vision for the future, and provided a unique opportunity to harness the knowledge, skills and life experiences of former soldiers, sailors, airmen and marines for the greater good of young people in schools. This book supports the aim of this programme very well.

Rob McDougall
Head of Learning and Development
SkillForce
December 2011

MENTORING IN SCHOOLS – THE WAY TO SUCCEED

Introduction

Every year of a young person's education is an important step on their path to becoming a valuable member of society. Every step they take is moving them nearer to living a happy and fulfilling life.

That is the ideal situation for our young people. However, it is not always the reality. Modern day life can present all sorts of challenges that young people have to cope with whilst they try to get a good education. Do we need to list them? NO!

No young person goes to school determined to fail and yet this can be the outcome for all too many these days. So what can be done to help young people to achieve despite the challenges that they may face?

Mentoring has for a long time been seen as a way of helping people to fulfil their potential.

Mentoring as a concept is not new. Historically the word 'mentor' originates from Greek mythology. Homer's Odyssey relates the story of King Odysseus, who on leaving to go to war, entrusted his son Telemachus to the care of his friend and advisor, Mentor. Mentor's job was not merely to raise Telemachus, but also to prepare him for the responsibilities he was to assume in his lifetime.

This book breaks Mentoring down into simple steps that will help you to succeed as a Mentor. We will look at:

- Support your Mentee
- Understand Mentoring and your Mentee
- Create a learning environment
- Challenge when necessary
- Encourage independence
- Evaluate progress
- Deliver results

Let's begin, however, with a recent exercise that was inspirational.

When working with the Military 2 Mentor initiative spearheaded by SkillForce, we asked what are some of the skills, qualities and experience that SkillForce Mentors bring to the role of Mentor? With predominantly military backgrounds, this extra-ordinary group of individuals came up with:

- Knowing right from wrong
- Punctuality
- Standards
- Loyalty
- Dedication
- Respect
- Consistency
- Persistence
- Courage
- Common Sense
- Self discipline
- Self reliance
- Self awareness
- Pride in appearance
- Honesty
- Integrity
- Communication Skills
- Endurance
- Trust
- Bravery
- Responsibility
- Caring
- Maturity
- Empathy
- Sense of humour
- Fun loving
- Stamina (mental & emotional)
- Reliability

- Leadership skills
- Decision making skills
- Honour
- Judgement
- Professionalism
- Team players

What a list!

When young people engage with the values and beliefs that these Mentors live their lives by, the impact on them is truly amazing. With a 'can do' attitude to life along with the support and encouragement of a Mentor, young people can come to realise that anything is possible.

So let's start at the beginning.

CHAPTER ONE

SUPPORT YOUR MENTEE

When you work as a Mentor in a school, you are working as part of a team, which can include:
- Form tutors
- Subject teachers
- Heads of Faculty
- Heads of Year
- Assistant Head Teachers
- Head Teacher
- Education Welfare Officer
- Learning Support Unit
- Child Protection Officer
- School counsellor
- Social workers
- Youth Workers

As part of this team, it is important to know what support you can call upon to achieve the best outcome for your Mentee.

However, supporting your Mentee effectively also requires an understanding of what mentoring is and isn't. Think back to a time when you made significant decisions or changes in your life. Whose opinions or help did you seek? What was it about them that encouraged you to seek their input?

You may have found someone who:
- Gave you encouragement
- Helped you build up your confidence
- Had relevant experience to share
- Was a positive role model
- You felt you could confide in

Mentoring incorporates all of the above and more. There are skills that are shared with non-directive coaching such as listening, questioning, summarising and offering feedback. Let's look at the similarities and differences in the Spectrum of Mentoring and Coaching below.

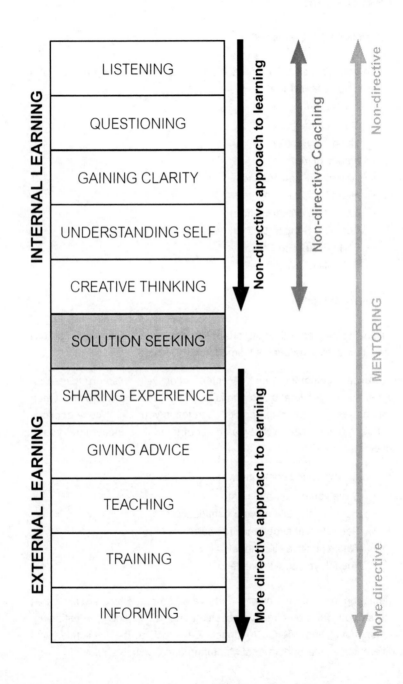

Mentoring covers the entire spectrum whereas a non-directive coaching approach would stay on the right hand side. Permission from the Coachee would be sought before entering the left hand side of 'solution seeking' and only then if the Coachee was finding difficulty in finding a way forward.

Mentoring vs Therapy
An important boundary to appreciate is that between mentoring and therapy. Mentoring is not therapy. Recognising when counselling would be a more appropriate intervention at a particular time is a responsibility of a Mentor. In the following table is a brief comparison between therapy and mentoring.

Therapy	Mentoring
Deals with identifiable dysfunctions in a person	Deals with a healthy Young Person desiring a better situation
Deals mostly with a person's past and trauma, and seeks healing	Deals mostly with a Young Person's present and seeks to help them design a more desirable future
Helps client resolve old pain	Helps Young Person learn new skills and tools to build a more satisfying successful future
Therapist-client relationship is more akin to doctor-patient	Co-creative partnership (Mentor helps the Young Person discover best way forward)
Deals with emotions that are still 'hooking' the client from the past	Can deal with difficult emotions but only if they are not still embedded in the past
The Therapist diagnoses, then provides professional expertise and guidelines to provide a path to healing	The Mentor stands with the Young Person and helps him or her identify the challenges, then partners to turn challenges into victories, holding the Young Person accountable to reach desired goals
Progress may sometimes be slow and possibly painful	Growth and progress may be achieved in a short period of time and it is hoped that the journey is enjoyable

What signals might flag up that counselling would be more supportive to a Mentee?

- Constantly dwelling in the past
- Constantly speaking negatively about themselves
- Unable to achieve simple goals consistently
- Signs of abuse (visit www.dcsf.gov.uk/everychildmatters)

In the event that you believe your Mentee requires the specialist skills of a counsellor, then understanding the appropriate reporting procedure in your school is important. Every School will also have a Child Protection Policy and you should have a copy.

Support your Mentee - the practicalities

The Role of a Mentor
Supporting the development of your Mentee can require you to adopt many different roles. These can include:

- Rapport builder
- Active listener
- Effective questioner
- Effective communicator
- Motivator
- Influencer
- A positive role model
- Solution seeker
- Resource provider

Consider also the skills, qualities and experience that **you** bring to your role as a Mentor.

Building rapport

Essential to supporting your Mentee effectively is the ability to build rapport. An English dictionary definition of rapport states 'a close and harmonious relationship in which the people involved understand each other's feelings and ideas.' The key words here are 'harmonious', which indicates a lack of conflict or stress, and 'understanding', which suggests that the people are on the same wavelength. When rapport is missing the quality of communication suffers, it can be impossible to gain agreement, achieve outcomes and feel respect for the other person. This is even more important when working with young people.

Rapport in any relationship includes a strong sense of trust and mutual respect that allows a free and honest exchange of views. Rapport can build naturally, provided there is some commonality between the two parties. This happens at an unconscious level. By appreciating exactly how this happens, we can choose to raise our awareness of this natural process.

Aspects of rapport – non-verbal communication

Non-verbal communication can play an interesting part in rapport. When somebody walks into a room, we may unconsciously notice body language – their physical appearance, posture and the clothes they are wearing. Within seconds we can start to make some assumptions about the kind of person they are and whether there is anything about them with which we can identify. If there is, we are more likely to want to get to know them. If there isn't, we may choose not to connect with them.

With young people, it may be necessary to make a conscious decision not to pre-judge them on appearance as they do belong to a different generation! Also, family background may have an impact on first impressions - family incomes vary enormously, for example. First impressions may belie the person underneath.

How do you know that rapport has been established?

Some key aspects include:

- Good eye contact
- Relaxed facial expression
- Similar body language
- Listening to each other
- Showing respect
- Similar values, beliefs

What can you do if you become aware that rapport is missing?

You do not want a young person to feel threatened, challenged or uncomfortable in any way. Nor do you want to provoke negative feelings. An awareness of your body language and the possible assumptions or interpretations that a young person may be making is important.

Hence adopting a neutral stance is helpful. By showing sincerity, genuine interest and empathy, you can diffuse or disarm potential hostility or alienation. Key elements of rapport are also trust and respect. One way to use your body language to convey these qualities is to keep it open. In many situations, an encouraging smile can also diffuse a potentially difficult situation.

Being aware of the language a young person uses can also help to build rapport. We can tell a lot about people from their choice of words. When we speak, we communicate in 'channels', visual, auditory, kinaesthetic (VAK). If you listen for the kinds of words that a young person uses, they are providing you with an indication of whether they are thinking in pictures, sounds or feelings. We will look at VAK in more detail in a later section.

ACTIVE LISTENING

Let's begin by considering listening versus hearing.

Hearing is defined in the Shorter Oxford dictionary as 'having a perception of sound' and listening is defined as 'to hear attentively'.

Here lies an interesting difference that can be useful in our understanding of the activity called listening.

When have you heard someone say, 'I hear you!' Often expressed with a certain tone of irritation designed to invite someone to stop communicating!

Have you come across the expression used in relation to listening 'only hearing what you want to hear'?

Active listening will be used to denote the type of listening that focuses on the speaker. Hearing refers more to the context of 'what does this mean for me' type of listening.

What happens when we begin to receive information from someone? The danger is that we automatically start to impose our own opinions and judgments on what we are hearing. Hence why hearing and listening can become two separate activities.

The gift of listening

Listening is one of the first skills that people focus on when learning to use mentoring skills, as it is so important to become a more effective communicator. When you listen with the intention of fully understanding, then there is an effect on a young person. Not only do they feel valued, but it also becomes easier to share the essence and meaning of their communication. They may even gain a better understanding themselves of what they wish to communicate as a result. Better understanding helps everyone to see a situation more clearly; to become more aware and ultimately to make better decisions or choices. Developing good listening skills can be a real asset in everyday life.

As children, our parents may have spent time and effort teaching us how to speak, to pronounce words, to be polite and to speak clearly.

However, although we were taught how to speak, how much time was spent teaching us how to listen? The outcome is that we may be able to hear rather than necessarily listen.

Listening is taken for granted in that we assume if we start to speak, someone is listening. They maybe hearing but not necessarily listening. How frustrating is it when you sense that the person that you are speaking to is not really listening to you?

How can you tell?

They may jump in at the earliest opportunity to talk about themselves in some way. At worst, maybe it is the fact that their eyes keep moving around the room to see who else is there, or their eyes glaze over. If someone is exposed to this 'non-listening' regularly, it can have a negative impact on their self-esteem. This is particularly relevant for young people. The message received is that they do not have anything of value to say which becomes translated into 'I have no value'.

So, where to start when we want to develop good listening skills?

Preparing to listen
If you think of listening as part of the foundation of effective mentoring, then the first step is to clear a space in just the same way you would if you were going to build a house. Living in the 21st century is so hectic for many people that having the space in your head to take on board any more information can be challenging. You only have to try and sit quietly for a minute to become aware of the huge number of thoughts that flash around in your mind. Creating a space is important in preparation for real listening to occur. This means taking control of our own thoughts so that we can focus on the person who is asking us to listen to them.

However, people are seeking to be listened to all day, every day, at home or at school. So how can we be ready to realistically listen effectively at any moment? An understanding of the situation and the speaker's needs are helpful initially. Casual communications occur throughout each day that may not require the same preparation as a more in depth conversation with a work colleague or family member. The nature of the topic will also help to determine the degree of preparation needed. Eventually, listening rather than hearing becomes second nature.

To begin with the following ideas may be useful, starting with two simple things that will enhance your general well-being anyway.

- Do some simple stretching exercises
- Simple meditation – find a comfortable place to sit and take a deep breath. Then focus on your natural breathing for a few minutes. Each time you breath out, imagine that you are letting go of your own thoughts and worries for a while. Be aware of letting go of any tension in your body at the same time
- Write out a 'to do' list so that you stop dwelling on what you have to do for a while
- Go for a short walk somewhere quiet

There are many ways of being prepared for listening. Experimenting to discover what works best for you can be fun. By creating your own inner space ready for listening to someone else has the effect of offering that young person some space also. When our heads are cluttered by thoughts, it is more challenging to think clearly. If the desired outcome of a communication is to make new connections, create new ideas and thoughts, then clearing a space in which this can happen is essential.

Being able to create and offer space needs practice but it is well worth the effort. The reward is enhanced communication, enriched relationships and greater creativity.

Barriers to listening
For listening as opposed to hearing to occur, it is essential that our own opinions and judgments are controlled or 'parked up' for a while. Everyone has his or her own opinions, beliefs and views of a particular topic or question. It is very easy as a listener to prejudge and interpret the speaker's words in terms of our own opinions. It is also common to respond and colour the conversation with our own opinions. An effective mentor can set aside their opinions in the first instance to listen with the intention of seeking to understand from another's point of view.

Experiences are our practical acquaintances with facts, feelings and events. As someone speaks, we may recognise a situation and will automatically start to hear what relates to our own experience, while making assumptions that the speaker's experience followed a similar pattern. However, their experience of a similar event may have been entirely different and in understanding their experience, an effective

Mentor maintains focus and listens to their Mentee. The discipline required here is not to interrupt and to understand the power of silence.

Nancy Kline, in her book Time to Think, emphasises this by saying that when the talking stops the thinking does not. When someone knows that you are truly listening to them and that you do not intend to interrupt them, a wealth of creative thinking can take place.

Summarising and reflecting back
Finally, the measure of how effectively you are listening can be gained through summarising and reflecting back what you have heard to your client. If you choose to paraphrase, then the accuracy of your interpretation can be gauged by the words that you may choose to use. If these vary from those used by your Mentee, then checking that the essence of the communication has remained in tact is essential. Otherwise you can end up 'putting words in the mouth' of your Mentee. This can result in dishonouring what your Mentee is wishing to share with you, which, in turn, may impoverish the quality of the communication and hence the relationship that exists between you.

Developing the qualities of a good listener
Some people seem to be naturally gifted with listening skills. However, it is important to recognise that the qualities of a good listener can be learned and enhanced by everyone. Six key qualities of a good listener are explored here, but there are doubtless other qualities.

Respect
An effective Mentor listens with respect for what a young person has to say. Even if slightly boring, or thinking that we have heard it all before; they may contradict what we think we know or believe to be true. A good listener resists the temptation to relapse into intolerant or non-listening. Whatever is being said at that moment is important to the speaker and an effective Mentor applies active and positive listening at all times. Effective communication is mutually beneficial and each party is entitled to respect from each other.

Genuine Interest

When we are listening to someone, we are not just acting the part. An effective Mentor demonstrates to their Mentee that they are really listening. A good listener shows that they are really interested, really care and are really committed to understanding what is being communicated.

Empathy

Seeing the world through your Mentee's eyes, means to 'feel with' them, rather than 'feel like' them. Effective communication is about listening to another's perspective. When someone knows that you understand at this level, they are much more likely to continue and take the conversation to deeper levels. This in turn enriches your interpersonal relationship.

Gaining clarity

You can listen to a young person expressing all sorts of vague notions and ideas. They may talk to you not knowing what they want to say exactly; indeed one thing that a young person may need help with is formulating their ideas. A good listener is able to clarify vague and muddled ideas through feeding back accurately what they hear and by asking questions that emerge from what they are listening to. This helps the young person to become more specific. Hence an effective Mentor shows clarity in their own thinking.

Mental agility

To expand on gaining clarity, a good listener will be able to reflect back the essence of the conversation, to succinctly describe the situation. In doing this, the effective Mentor is feeding back to the young person what they have said. This alone often helps them to see a situation differently perhaps. For example, it may enable them to see an unwanted truth. Understanding the dynamics of the conversation, knowing where you are at a particular point, requires practice. 'Dancing in the moment' describes this well.

Timing

Finally, timing is knowing when to ask a question or when to remain silent; when and how it may be helpful to interrupt.

The use of silence

Let us explore the use of silence a little more. In ordinary conversations a period of silence can be uncomfortable. The person feeling most uncomfortable will seek to fill the gap. Within effective communication, silence can be natural – there is no pressure, the Mentor is there to listen when the young person is ready.

Silence allows uninterrupted thinking time and gives the young person the opportunity to make new connections in their mind, which can lead to new thinking patterns. As the listener, there are many ways to interpret silence. The young person may have become distracted or bored, feel depressed or disinterested. He or she may also be in a reflective mood. If the Mentor is listening with empathy and intuition, then understanding the nature of the silence is easier, which can draw an appropriate response from the listener – to speak or not to speak.

Interrupting

However, when is it appropriate to interrupt? Some people can talk continuously! They may have good reason in that they need to unload information or emotions; maybe the subject is long and complicated. Equally the young person may be trying to avoid considering an issue; trying to impress you; they may have become bogged down in descriptive detail or feel uneasy about silence. None of this supports effective communication.

An effective Mentor needs to be careful before interrupting. Sometimes what seems irrelevant can be a roundabout way of the speaker getting to what they need to say. Hence the need to decide whether you are listening to aimless rambling and repetition or whether there is a positive benefit likely to come from going along with the young person. If not, then an effective Mentor intervenes respectfully. The easiest way to do this is to establish an understanding in the relationship that permits you to interrupt in order to move the conversation on more positively.

QUESTIONING TECHNIQUES

What is a question?
'A sentence worded or expressed so as to obtain information.' Oxford English Dictionary. In conversation with another person, a question asked is an invitation from you to that person. The invitation is to share information or an opinion. Different types of question (e.g. open or closed) can be viewed simply as sending different invitations. The skill in asking questions is to think of the type of response you seek and then choose the appropriate invitation. Being conscious of the power of questions and developing your ability to use them effectively will enhance your interpersonal relationships – a vital part of becoming an effective Mentor.

What impact does a question have?
When a person is asked a question, the brain naturally responds by seeking an answer. Hence when an effective question is posed, this can trigger a significant search for the appropriate answer, particularly if it is an open question.

As you develop your abilities in asking effective questions, remember to practice your use of silence. This offers your listener sufficient time to formulate an answer that will be of value to you and them. With knowledge comes responsibility. In this case, the responsibility is to be aware of the power of questions. Unlike non-directive coaching, it can become the function of a Mentor to direct a young person's thinking through the questions they choose to ask. From effective listening however, the questions that would best serve to ask at any given moment still frequently emerge from what has just been said or not said.

Questions are powerful
In everyday conversation people usually ask questions to get information that they want to use. However, when asking questions as a Mentor, the point of asking a question can be to invite the young person to think in new ways. The questions posed can be like a guided voyage of discovery for their benefit.

Probing questions can challenge current thinking, direct attention, open new perspectives, halt evasion and gain clarification.

Different types of question

One aspect of the role of a Mentor is to raise awareness. It goes without saying that this is their own awareness as well as that of others.

Other aspects which all have this dual impact are:

- To encourage clarity
- To challenge thinking
- To invite ownership

Through listening a Mentor challenges perceptions – their own as well as that of others. A single word can achieve this very effectively. For example, when a Mentee is talking in generalisations.'

Mentee: *'Nobody likes me.'*

Mentor: *'Nobody?'*

Can you hear how you would say it? This may produce confirmation of 'nobody' which could open up a dialogue. On the other hand it may produce evidence that contradicts the perception. This again provides useful information to inform further dialogue.

Mentee: *I always mess up.'*

Mentor: *'Always?'*

Again, the response will inform. If it is 'well, nearly always', the next question can be:

Mentor: *'When was the last time you did not mess up?'*

A single word can make a very useful question.

Open & Closed Questions

Closed questions seek specific information, often requiring simply a 'yes' or 'no' response. Open questions are open for the young person to choose the appropriate level of detail and the exact nature of the response. This often leads to a fuller answer, as open questions tend to invite the young person to think a little more about the subject - they open up the thinking process.

Examples:

Question: *'Did you do your homework?'*

This is a classic closed question inviting a simple 'yes' or 'no' response. It is possible for the young person to give more information about whether he did or did not, but this would be an answer to a follow up question that has yet to be asked.

Question: *'How did you get on with your homework?'*

This question is sending a positive message that you believe they did their homework and opens up the dialogue more.

Question: *'Were you sent out of your music lesson?'*

Again this is a closed question seeking very specific information and may get a very short answer!

Question: *'What was your reaction to being sent out of music?'*

This is an open question that is raising awareness and begins to invite the young person to own their behaviour.

Question: *'What happened that ended up with you being sent out of your music lesson?'*

This is an open question that asks the young person to explore their behaviour.

Question: *'What went through your mind as you were asked to leave the room?'*

This is an open question that asks a person to start exploring their values and beliefs.

If you check your anticipated response from the question you are about to ask and it is yes or no, this clearly indicates that you are about to ask a closed question.

If this is not your intention or useful at this time, how can you alter it quickly to open it up? If you simply choose one of the question starters from the list below this is usually suficient:

Who, what, when, where, how and which?

Probing questions

Probing questions invite the respondent to reflect upon their own knowledge, experience, values and opinions to find an answer that honours them. They offer a young person the opportunity to hear themselves working out what they want to do and how they are going to do it.

In some situations, effective mentoring is all about supporting young people to be very specific about what they want to say, what they are going to do and when they are going to do it. So probing questions can tie things down.

Question: *'What are you going to do differently that ensures that your report form is signed positively?'*

Positive, optimistic messages

A Mentor believes in their Mentee and their ability to achieve whatever they want. This is a very powerful part of mentoring, which encourages and supports someone to achieve. Here are some examples of questions a Mentor might ask with a brief explanation of the positive, optimistic message within the question.

Question: *'What did you learn from that experience?'*

There was something valuable to learn from the experience.

Question: *'What resources do you need to acquire to achieve this goal?'*

There are resources that you are capable of accessing and you can achieve your goal.

Be guided by your intention

The intention of sharing with you different types of question is not to overwhelm you or concern you about asking the 'right' type of question! An increased awareness of the power that questions can have is designed to enhance your effectiveness as a Mentor. Always be guided by your own intuition and your intention with asking any question.

THE SKILLS OF GIVING AND RECEIVING FEEDBACK

The skills of giving and receiving feedback are fundamental to effective relationships and mentoring, as you will be required to give and receive feedback throughout the mentoring process.

Giving Feedback
To support your Mentee to maintain or develop their performance, your feedback should be:

Specific
Pointing out several examples of good performance as well as highlighting detailed examples of the particular occasions where there is scope for improvement.

Immediate
Feedback is given constructively at the moment it is necessary.

Relevant
Relevant to aspects of performance, and not directed to the Mentee as a person.

Helpful
Concentrating on behaviour, which can be changed and seeking alternatives.

Non-judgmental
Describing unhelpful or unproductive behaviour rather than criticising it.

Non-directive
As far as possible, help your Mentee to discover their own solutions and choices.

Forward Looking
The feedback should not dwell on the negative aspects of past performance, but look to the future and developing solutions and choices.

Not only related to problems
Include praise and positive support for successes.

A quick feedback model that can also be useful is **BBC**

- **B**alanced – avoid emotive language
- **B**elievable – base feedback only on facts, not supposition
- **C**onstructive – encouraging positive actions to be taken

Feedback needs to be a two way process in mentoring. Hence asking for feedback is important too.

Receiving Feedback
Receiving feedback is equally important. When you ask a young person for feedback on how you are mentoring them, it not only gives them the opportunity to share how they feel about the relationship they are developing with you, it also sends the message that you value them and their opinions. A few essentials here include:

- Receive feedback as a gift that provides you with honest information about your perceived behaviour/performance. Be open to what you will hear.
- When feedback is positive, accept it gracefully.
- Let the young person finish what he or she is saying.
- Ask for specifics, if not provided.
- Ask the young person to give you alternatives to your behaviour.
- Thank the young person for being helpful to you.
- Take the time after the feedback interaction to evaluate the information and consider specific actions for improvements.
- Don't take it personally.
- Don't brush is off with misplaced humour or sarcasm.
- Don't put your self down.
- Don't become defensive or explain your behaviour. (You can either spend your time mobilising your defences or you can spend your time listening. Defending your actions is counterproductive, where listening is extremely useful).

SUPPORT GOAL SETTING

When a young person comes to mentoring, they may have been sent by their school or have requested mentoring support. Either way, they may have goals or targets that have been set by the school or they will be setting their own.

If they have goals or targets that have been set for them, then the first conversation is to check that they are in agreement with them. If not, you need to support them to 'buy in' to these targets. Breaking down the targets into appropriate and agreed learning outcomes that are ultimately stated in the words of the young person is essential. For example:

School Target
- Punctuality

Learning   outcomes
- Strategies to arrive at school on time

Personal statements to support learning outcomes
- *'I can get out of bed by 7.30am.'*
- *'I can catch the bus by 8.30am.'*
- *'I can arrive at school on time.'*

However, if you find yourself in a situation where knowing where to start is the issue you may find the following exercise useful. It is called the Eight Fundamentals and we have found it a valuable way to start a mentoring relationship on many occasions. We offer it to you as part of your mentoring toolkit.

THE EIGHT FUNDAMENTALS

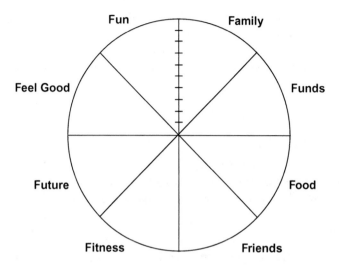

When the eight sections represented above are in balance, then life flows.

Regard the centre of the wheel as 0 and the outer edge as 10, estimate how happy they are within each area of their life – 0 being not very happy to 10 being very happy.

Draw a straight line between each section to create a new outer edge. The new perimeter of the circle represents their current position.

If this were a real wheel, how bumpy would the ride through their life be?

When working with The Eight Fundamentals, we have listed below some examples of the types of questions you could pose in each section to stimulate your Mentee's thinking.

Future
- *How happy are you with your school work?*
- *How happy are you with your personal development?*
- *How happy are you with your ambitions?*
- *How happy are you with your job prospects?*
- *How happy do you feel with the way your future is shaping up?*

Funds
This section relates to their relationship with money:

- *How do you get money?*
- *How do you spend money?*
- *How do you manage your money?*
- *How happy are you with the way you think about money?*

Family
- *How happy are you with the relationship that you have with your family?*

Friends
- *How happy are you with the friends you have?*

Fun
- *How much fun do you have in your life?*

Food
- *How happy are you with your relationship with food?*

Fitness
- *How happy are you with your level of fitness?*

Feel Good Factor
- *What things do you do each day that make you feel good about yourself?*

Once you have supported your Mentee to complete this exercise, their wheel might look like this:

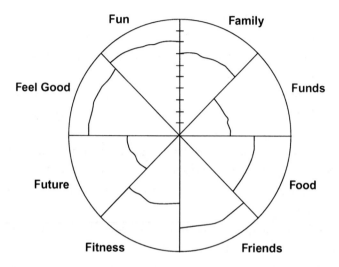

You then have a point of discussion and a place to start depending on which section they choose to address first. The next question can then be:

- *So what do you want to achieve/change about …..?*

Let's finish this chapter with a lighthearted look at how not to Mentor compiled by David Clutterbuck.

12 Habits of a Toxic Mentor

1. Start from the point of view that you - from your vast experience and broader perspective - know better than the Mentee what's in his or her best interest

2. Be determined to share your wisdom with them - whether they want it or not; remind them frequently how much they still have to learn

3. Decide what you and the Mentee will talk about and when; change dates and themes frequently to prevent complacency sneaking in

4. Do most of the talking; check frequently that they are paying attention

5. Make sure they understand how trivial their concerns are compared to the weighty issues you have to deal with

6. Remind the Mentee how fortunate they are to have your undivided attention

7. Neither show nor admit any personal weaknesses; expect to be their role model in all aspects of career development and personal values

8. Never ask them what they should expect of you - how would they know anyway?

9. Demonstrate how important and well connected you are by sharing confidential information they don't need (or want) to know

10. Discourage any signs of levity or humour - this is a serious business and should be treated as such

11. Take them to task when they don't follow your advice

12. Never, never admit that this could be a learning experience for you, too.

CHAPTER TWO

UNDERSTANDING THE MENTORING CYCLE AND UNDERSTAND-
ING YOUR MENTEE

In this chapter we will look at the Mentoring Cycle and how this understanding can support you to achieve a natural rhythm in your mentoring. We will also explore what knowledge you can access about your Mentee that can support you to mentor them more effectively.

Let's begin with the Mentoring Cycle. This looks at the preparation a Mentor can do prior to entering into the mentoring relationship, right through to concluding an agreement. This is best summed up by the following diagram.

THE MENTOR CYCLE

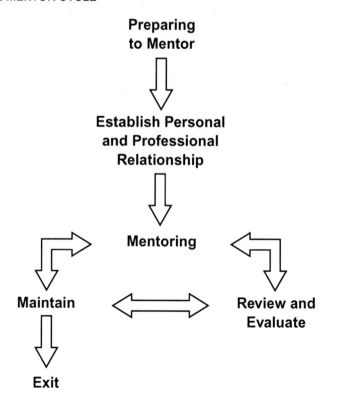

Preparing to Mentor

The work that you can do prior to entering into mentoring can be critical to the smooth running of the relationship with a young person. Information should include:

- Having background information about the young person
- An understanding of the role and scope of mentoring
- An understanding of the support structure within the school
- An understanding of the reporting structure in the school

What the young person is coming to mentoring for is useful but you may not know that until they arrive at their first session.

However, young people seek mentoring for a variety of reasons, such as:

- Improving classroom behaviour
- Being more engaged in their learning experience
- Improving punctuality
- Improving attendance
- Building self esteem
- Dealing with transition & change
- Releasing potential
- Dealing with bullying
- Enhancing educational performance
- Supporting the gifted and talented
- Dealing with family break down
- Making decisions about their future

What is an appropriate environment in which to mentor?

One which is:

- Quiet
- Not overheard (maintains confidentiality)
- Convenient location in the school
- Not isolated
- Adheres to Health & Safety requirements
- Adheres to Child Protection Policy
- Visible

In summary, a private space in a public place.

If you find that the environment is not conducive to a successful mentoring session, then negotiate a better location with the school!

Establishing the personal relationship

We have already looked at building rapport, which is fundamental to establishing the personal relationship with your Mentee. A relationship that is built on trust enables you to better understand your Mentee and for them to gain the maximum from the time they spend with you. Where there is trust between a Mentor and Mentee, there is tremendous strength. How does trust become established and sustained in a relationship? The word itself can be used as a helpful aide-memoire.

Truth

Respect

Understanding

Space

Time

Truth

That sounds obvious or simple enough you may be thinking. But is it? Over the years phrases such as 'being economic with the truth' have become part of our culture. Sometimes, it can be a case of not wishing to hurt someone's feelings or thinking 'what they don't know won't hurt them'. From a Mentor's perspective it could be a situation where you have promised to do something but you have over-committed yourself.

Creating an environment where a young person can be totally truthful gives them the opportunity to really make changes and move forward in their lives. For example, when they can talk truthfully about what is working about the way they choose to behave and what is not working about the way they choose to behave, then they have taken ownership of who they are choosing to be.

As a Mentor do you need to be liked or do you want to be respected? There is an important distinction. Since you may need to challenge your Mentee on occasions and if you draw back from that point of truth, you are not serving your Mentee, you are colluding with them. The issue is yours.

Without being judgemental, but simply being truthful, you can encourage your Mentee to take responsibility and choose to change.

Being non-judgemental and unconditional is vital when you are working with young people as this encourages them to speak their truth without fear of being thought less of.

Mentoring works in the present, which eliminates the need for excuses. It supports a young person to think 'this is where I am right now – where do I want to go from here and how do I intend to get there?'

Being truthful and positive builds respect between you and your Mentee.

Respect

By respecting others, you gain respect. It is important not to come to the mentoring relationship with the approach that you know what is best for your Mentee. This type of behaviour is difficult to interrupt, since it is done in the name of being supportive and 'on their side'. It is subtle and unconscious. 'I just want the best for you, that's all.' We can't do this to a young person and give him or her profound levels of respectful attention at the same time.

Respect is enhanced with openness and honesty. Respecting a young person's values and beliefs builds a strong relationship. Every young person is a unique individual and recognising this diversity, respecting the differences that individuals possess, are important steps in establishing the personal relationship with your Mentee.

Understanding

Mentoring assists you to understand a young person's values and beliefs. When you show you understand, you are interacting in a way that honours them. This is turn can enhance their self-esteem.

Showing a young person that you genuinely want to understand what matters to them and how they feel develops a strong foundation to the relationship. In this sense it is akin to empathy.

However, notice the difference between understanding how a young person might be feeling and believing that you know how they feel.

It is not possible to know exactly how another person is feeling. Even if you have had a similar experience, each person's experience is unique to them. This is particularly important as a Mentor where sharing experience can be part of your role.

When supporting a young person to understand themselves better, it is important to create the right space and to give them space.

Space

Physical, mental and emotional space are all equally important when a young person is challenging themselves to make real changes in their lives.

We have looked at the ideal physical environment for mentoring to take place. Creating mental and emotional space can be a simple process of offering to listen without interrupting while your Mentee 'empties out stuff'. Let us repeat that when a young person is truly listened to, they feel valued and validated.

There is another aspect to space that is valuable to appreciate and that is the space inside our heads. What does a young person listen to inside their heads that does not serve them well, such as limiting and negative beliefs that emerge as negative self-talk? Dealing with negative beliefs and self-talk is explored in the chapters 'Challenging when necessary' and 'Encouraging Independence'.

However, real people can also invade this inner space. They listen to a young person's dreams only in order to try and take them away i.e 'dream stealers'. Also for young people there is the challenge of peer group pressure. Some young people are facing a culture of 'it's not cool to want to learn'. Their inner space is dominated by the need to be accepted by their peers rather than creating a special space where they can plan and work towards a rewarding future.

Mentoring is about creating that space both externally and internally that supports a young person to realise and release their full potential.

Time

There is a great deal of discussion these days about how time poor the average family is. This has nothing to do with financial poverty.

Time poverty can occur simply because both parents or carers are working long hours and are too tired to engage properly with their children when they finally get home. A recent survey highlighted by 'Super Nanny' Jo Frost, suggested that the average time that an adult spends with their child is just 49 minutes per day. Some people walk their dogs longer than that.

Giving a young person the feeling that when they spend time with you, that they are the most important person to you at that moment is very powerful. Hence why it is so important to prepare to listen, so that you can give them your undivided attention. For some this may be a new experience. Not interrupting so that they have time to think and say all that they want or need to say is equally powerful. Nancy Kline in her book 'Time to Think' talks about how we learn at a very young age to say what we want to say in 30 seconds as we learn that after this time we will be interrupted. As mentioned before, she also talks about when the talking stops, the thinking does not. So giving a young person the time and space to explore their thoughts can support them to discover and create a fulfilling future for themselves.

A final thought about time. There is no such thing as time management! There is only self-management. This is another important area where mentoring can support a young person.

Having begun to establish the personal relationship with your Mentee, it is important to establish the professional relationship. This may or may not happen in the first session. That will depend on your Mentee and the time that it may take to build rapport and lay the foundations of the personal relationship. However, it is important to set out the guidelines and agreements for the professional relationship.

Establishing the professional relationship

The aim here is to ensure that your Mentee:

- Understands how mentoring works including confidentiality
- Understands the expectations both of the Mentee and of the Mentor
- Understands the boundaries of mentoring.
- Agrees the practicalities of the mentoring sessions

So initially, it may be useful to talk briefly about your philosophy of mentoring. This may be something as simple as:

'I believe in your ability to achieve and I am here to support you and encourage you to do so.'

In describing the mentoring process, just put your cards on the table. The following may stimulate ideas.

'I am not here to tell you what to do as I believe that you can work that out for yourself with my support.'

'I am here to listen to you and to offer you questions that will help you to work out what is best for you.'

'I am not here to judge you.'

'I will ask permission to interrupt you if I think that you are wandering off the point or if I hear you talking negatively about yourself.'

'I will share my experiences, offer guidance and information only if they could be helpful to you. That will be for you to decide.'

'Anything you say to me will be in confidence. You will know what information goes on your school record i.e. when we meet, how long our sessions are, the targets you are working towards and your progress.'

Understanding the expectations might include:

'My expectations of you are that you will be open and honest with me and work with me in our sessions together.'

Ask what their expectations are of you.

'I will offer you feedback and I want you to give me feedback as well.'

Regarding boundaries, it is important to say that you are not a counsellor and if anything should come up in your sessions together that you are not qualified to deal with then you will seek the right support for them.

N.B. You are legally required to report any concerns/disclosures about child abuse to the school's Child Protection Officer. Under no circumstances do you attempt an investigation or offer your Mentee complete confidentiality. Your responsibility would be to complete a report and submit it within 24 hours to the relevant member of staff at the school.

Finally, there are the practicalities to agree such as where to meet, when to meet, how often, for how long. It is important also to consider how long the relationship itself is destined to last, so that both parties will recognise how and when it will end.

Then after asking if they have any questions – away you go!

Mentoring

The aim of a first official mentoring session is to create the opportunity for your Mentee to have a frank discussion on all matters concerning them. Establishing a pattern for the session is useful and we will go into more detail with examples of models that may be useful in the next chapter 'Creating a learning environment.'

Discussing and agreeing appropriate targets is an important first step in mentoring so that everyone knows what is being aimed for.

However, just talking to them is all that is needed to get the session under way and depending on what you have understood from your initial meeting it may be simply a case of asking them:

- *What makes you happy?*
- *What makes you sad?*
- *What makes you angry?*

Your Mentee may or may not have targets set to work towards. If they do, they may have been set by the school. If this is the case, then checking that they agree these targets is important otherwise they may not engage in the process. Again, having a frank discussion is needed to encourage them to engage.

If they are coming to mentoring and are setting their own targets then coaching them to set these targets is your role and the models in the next chapter will give you some ideas as to how to structure such a session.

Once targets are established, then your role is to encourage and support your Mentee to break them down into agreed learning outcomes and then achievable personal statements to keep encouraging themselves. For example:

Target

- Behaviour in class

Learning outcomes
- *What they can do in order to remain in class*
- *How to deal with feeling aggressive*
- *Understanding consequences of behaviour*

Personal statements to support Learning Outcomes
- *I can work positively in class*
- *I can work with others in class*
- *I can concentrate in class*
- *I can control my anger*
- *I understand that if I shout out in class, I will get a detention.*

At the end of a session it is important to check that your Mentee feels complete with the discussion and that they summarise what they are going to do/work on before your next session. Deciding how best to capture what has been agreed is part of the process. Writing things down or recording them in some way is important. Even signing a simple contract works well. Targets/personal statements can be carried around by a young person to encourage them, each day, to move one step closer to their target.

Review and evaluation

At the beginning of each subsequent session, it is valuable to review what has happened since you last met. The purpose of a review is to ensure that:

- Success are identified and acknowledged
- Improved performance is identified
- Problems can be identified and solutions sought
- Mentees gain recognition
- Mentors give and receive feedback

Evaluating is also an on-going process that should be happening between you and your Mentee as a natural part of your relationship in order to:

- Reflect on what has happened and why
- Evaluate progress towards targets
- Plan for future learning experiences
- Evaluate level of new thinking, knowledge, skills and understanding
- Evaluate how what they have learnt from mentoring will help them in the future

Mentors can review their performance.

Maintaining or concluding the relationship

This is the point in the cycle where the relationship either continues or ends clearly. If the relationship is to continue, then the review and evaluation will have highlighted this. Perhaps an original target has been achieved but there is now another that would benefit from mentoring support. So the mentoring continues.

On the other hand the mentoring relationship will end because:

- The Mentee has achieved all their targets
- The Mentee is working successfully and independently

It is important to acknowledge and celebrate all the success of the process and relationship before implementing an exit strategy.

Exit strategies

You need to consider an appropriate exit strategy with a young person rather than an abrupt end to the relationship e.g.

- Continue to review Mentee progress half-termly
- Offer contact in drop-in sessions
- Offer lunchtime/after school club attendance only
- Limit contact to meet and greet at break times, before school etc.
- Discuss young person's own preference for exit strategy

Finally, there may be an occasion when it will end for other reasons:

- The mentoring is not serving the Mentee
- The Mentee is becoming dependent on the relationship
- The mentoring relationship has broken down

In this situation, it is in no-one's interest to try and continue with something that is obviously not working, and both parties need to be honest with each other if they are unhappy in any way.

Supervision is an important part of the Mentor's work and can be helpful in these circumstances. Ensuring that the best interests of the young person are maintained is paramount.

UNDERSTAND CHANGE

James Prochaska and Carlo DiClemente's work on the Stages of Change shows that change is not as simple as many people assume. If it were, then we would all achieve our New Year's resolutions wouldn't we! They indicate that change takes time because there are six stages to change, one of which is 'relapse' and that is normal!

Understanding at which point a young person may be on the Change Model when they come to you can help you to know how best to proceed to help them arrive at a successful change.

Prochaska and DiClemente - Stages of Change Model

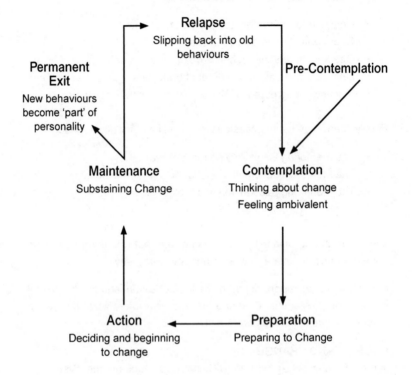

Stage of change	Where I am at
Pre-contemplation	I haven't been thinking about making changes and I don't intend to in the future.
Contemplation	I have thought about making changes but haven't actually done anything about it yet.
Preparation	I am intending to make a change or I have just started to make a change.
Action	I have been actively making changes for a short time.
Maintenance	I have been actively making noticeable changes for some time now.
Relapse	I had started to make changes but I have gone back to what I used to do.

The House of Change

Anthony Grant, Director of the Coaching Psychology Unit at the University or Sydney devised a model to show how thoughts affect feelings or attitude, which in turn impact on behaviour and actions, ultimately affecting performance. This is also useful to understand as a Mentor.

In the 'house', all dimensions must be aligned to maximise a young person's chances of reaching their targets.

The House of Change

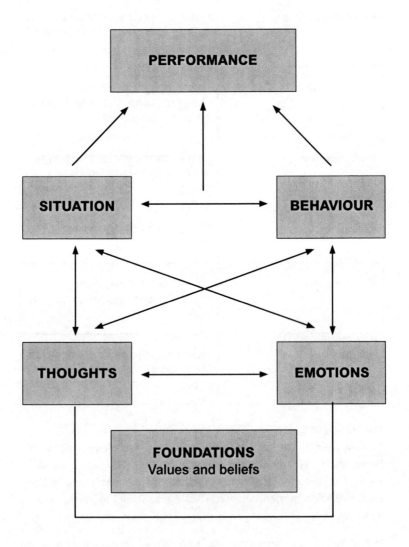

Adapted from The House of Change, Dr A Grant, 2002

UNDERSTAND YOUR MENTEE

Young people have different learning and communication styles, characterised by the way they take in and process information, and then communicate with others. The actual vocabulary they use represents an important part of communication. You can tell a lot about a young person from their choice of words.

We communicate in 'channels', visual, auditory, kinaesthetic, abbreviated to VAK. If you listen for the kinds of words that a young person uses when they are talking, they are providing you with an indication of whether they are thinking in pictures, sounds or feelings.

For example:

This phrase indicates that a visual person is speaking:

'I see what you mean.'

This is typical language used by an auditory person:

'I hear what you're saying.'

A kinaesthetic person speaking might say:

'I get what you're saying.'

Some schools help young people and teachers to become aware of their preferences to maximise the effectiveness of communication. If you are mentoring in a school where this is not the case then you could discover for yourself by offering the VAK questionnaire to your Mentee which is readily available as a free resource on the Internet.

Multiple Intelligences

'Every child is a genius until they are convinced otherwise.'

Pam Richardson 2004

Young people possess unlimited potential. However, from a school point of view this may not lie in literacy and numeracy.

Multiple intelligences have been recognised by many people working in the area of learning and personal development. Notable among them Dr. Howard Gardner, Professor of Education at Harvard University; Daniel Goleman (author of the book Emotional Intelligence) and Danah Zohar (co-author of the book Spiritual Intelligence). They suggest that the traditional notion of intelligence, based on I.Q. testing, is far too limited. Instead, nine different intelligences are proposed to account for a broader range of human potential in children and adults.

These intelligences are:

- **Literacy** – How comfortable is a young person with words, reading and writing?
- **Numeracy** – Does a young person enjoy numbers, logical, systematic thinking?
- **Spatial intelligence** – Can they see the whole picture, visualise an outcome?
- **Physical intelligence** – Are they well co-ordinated, naturally good at physical activities?
- **Musical intelligence** – Do they have an appreciation of sound and the effect on human emotion?
- **Interpersonal intelligence** – do they get on well with others, display natural empathy?
- **Intrapersonal intelligence** – how well do they know and understand themselves?
- **Natural intelligence** – do they possess an awareness of the inter-connectedness of humans and their environment?
- **Spiritual Intelligence** – do they sense that the physical world is not all that there is?

It is thought that people dominate in at least three intelligences. However, standard school tests in the early years tend to concentrate only on Literacy and Numeracy. What happens if a young person does not favour those intelligences?

David Beckham clearly shines in Spatial, Physical and Interpersonal Intelligences. Hence part of your role is to encourage a young person to acknowledge what they are good at and not what they are not good at. An awareness of the idea of multiple intelligences may assist you here. If you want to explore this with a Mentee, then Google multiple intelligences and a good website is displayed from Birmingham Grid for Learning – Multiple Intelligences. The results are presented online as an attractive multi-coloured pie chart, which can then be printed out. Encouraging your Mentee to comment on the findings can be a very fruitful self-esteem building exercise.

Finally let's explore how to encourage a young person to build their self-esteem. All too often, we have found that self-esteem is an issue. In today's world, young people need to leave school with strong self-belief and high self-esteem to manage the challenges and changes that they will face in the world of work.

Building self-esteem

Young people who feel good about themselves seem to have an easier time handling change or conflicts and resisting negative pressures. They tend to smile more readily and enjoy life. They are realistic and generally optimistic.

In contrast, young people with low self-esteem can find challenges to be sources of major anxiety and concern. Those who think poorly of themselves have a hard time finding solutions to problems. If their self-talk includes statements such as *'I'm no good'* or *'I always mess up,'* they may become passive, withdrawn, or depressed. Faced with a new challenge, their immediate response is *'I can't.'* Asked a question, their response is usually *'I don't know'*.

What young people believe about themselves from what others have told them may bear little relation to their true ability. So encouraging a young person to self-acknowledge can be a very rewarding activity for them. Asking them to consider the following can start this process off:

- *What makes you special?*
- *What are you good at?*
- *What makes you unique?*
- *What are you grateful for?*

Dealing with negative self-talk or limiting self-beliefs is dealt with in the chapter on 'Challenge when necessary'.

CHAPTER THREE

CREATING A LEARNING ENVIRONMENT

Bob Garvey and Kim Langridge in their book 'Pupil Mentoring' describe mentoring as 'a learning and development relationship' and that it involves following a process.

In this chapter we will explore a few models that can support the process of creating a learning environment in which a young person can thrive.

The mentoring conversation is a dynamic one designed to move a young person forward in their lives. Hence it is the responsibility of the Mentor to ensure that the conversation does not revert to a social conversation without achieving positive outcomes with the Mentee. How can this be achieved? Choosing a simple structure for each session can be very helpful.

HELP © *Jon Colley 2011*

Hello and welcome – sort out practicalities
Establish ground rules – refer to establishing the professional relationship
Listen to Mentee
Plan future actions with the Mentee (use GROW model)

This simple model is effective if you are new to mentoring. We will explore the **GROW** model in more detail. This is a useful tool to support effective goal setting.

FUNN

Find Out
Understand
Negotiate
Navigate

This model is highlighting how you can delve a little deeper into the mentoring conversation to elicit more learning with your Mentee.

The notion of 'a friend' has different meanings depending on a young person's view of life and their beliefs. By implementing the **FUNN** model, mentoring can be used to raise awareness and invite ownership of the role that your Mentee is choosing to play in their 'friends' sector. Below are some of the questions you could ask at each step of the **FUNN** Model during the exploration.

Finding out
- *What does the word 'friend' mean to you?*
- *What do you appreciate about your friends?*
- *What does it take to be a good friend?*

Understanding
- *What is working about your friendships?*
- *What is not working about your friendships?*
- *What do you want to change in the way that you are with your friends?*

Negotiating
- *Understanding what you want to change, what are you prepared to do?*
- *What are you not prepared to do?*
- *Who else do you need to negotiate with to bring about this change?*
- *What will you say?*

Navigating
- *What are you planning to do?*
- *How can you measure your progress?*
- *What obstacles might appear?*
- *How will you navigate around these?*

GROW

The **GROW** Model is a four-step process, described by John Whitmore in his book 'Coaching For Performance'. The model has proven its worth over many years, in the coaching profession, as a means of keeping focus in the coaching conversation. As we have already seen when mentoring you are inevitably also coaching. The aim of this model is to keep focus to achieve a positive outcome and a known way forward. Below is a simple demonstration of how this model could work in a mentoring conversation.

Goal

- *What specifically do you **really** want to achieve?*

Check that their goal is expressed in the

- Positive
- Personal
- Present tense

'I can arrive at school on time each day.'

Reality

- *What is the current situation in more detail?*
- *What have you done so far?*
- *What effect did this have?*
- *What support do you want?*

Options

- *What can you do to move one step towards your goal?*
- *How many different ideas can you come up with?*
- *If you knew you could do anything, what would you do?*

Way forward

- *Which option inspires you most?*
- *What are you actually going to do?*
- *When are you going to do it?*
- *What obstacles could get in the way?*
- *How can you overcome this?*
- *Who can support you?*
- *What do you want them to do?*
- *What conversation needs to happen? When? What will you say?*
- *How will you celebrate?*

This example has a distinct non-directive approach, which can work well to encourage a young person to engage in the process. The message is that they know what is best for them and that they are capable of finding their own way forward. This approach can also be used to build self-esteem.

MENTOR

John Richardson created The **MENTOR** model in 2006 to give more time to the goal setting phase of mentoring and coaching. When mentoring trainee Mentors, we were frequently finding that the G in GROW was being passed over too quickly as people wanted to get into talking about their issues immediately. Then at the end of a session if the question was posed 'what was the goal?' neither Mentee nor Mentor were able to state the goal that was being worked towards!

The **MENTOR** model gives a second opportunity to clearly define a goal. The initial goal can be outlined in 'Map out the Territory' but if it is not as clearly defined as it needs to be before a young person embarks on working out how best to achieve their goal, then the 'Negotiate' section provides this space.

- **M**ap out the territory
- **E**xplore the territory
- **N**egotiate the goals
- **T**hink tank time
- **O**ptions
- **R**ealisation and review

How might this work in practice?

Map out the Territory

Aim:

- to get a general overview or picture of the Mentee's reasons for entering into a mentoring relationship

Some Mentees may have requested mentoring, others may have been told that they are going to be mentored. Understanding where they are coming from is vital at the outset.

Questions could include:

- *'What do you want to achieve in the time we spend together?'* – **First session**.
- *'What do you want to achieve in today's session?'* – **Subsequent sessions**.

Explore the relationship in the first session

Explore the territory in subsequent sessions

Aim:

- to clarify the objectives of the mentoring
- to build rapport
- to explain the mentoring relationship i.e. confidentiality
- to agree the practicalities of the mentoring i.e. where, when

This is the contracting session initially and then becomes a review of what has been achieved from a previous session.

- *'What is going on at the moment?'*
- *'What has been working for you?'*

Negotiate Goals /Targets

Aim:

- to support, encourage and challenge thinking
- to discover what level of awareness and ownership of themselves/ their behaviours/attitudes they have
- to agree specific goals or targets

Questions could include:

- *'What are your long/short-term goals/targets in more detail?'*
- *'What are you prepared to do?'*
- *'What are you not prepared to do?'*
- *'Who can support you?'*

Applying **SMART** can be helpful as goals or targets need to be measurable and given a specific time frame in order to be achieved.

Think-Tank-Time
Aim:

- to put experience and knowledge on the table from both sides

This is a creative thinking opportunity. Questions could include:

- *'How are they going to achieve their goals/targets?'*
- *'What needs to happen for you to achieve your goals/targets?'*
- *'What have you tried?'*
- *'What haven't you tried?'*
- *'Again, who can support you?'*

This reinforces that they are not on their own when looking to achieve a goal. However, the discipline is to ask for help when it is needed.

Options
Aim:

- to make sense of outcomes from the previous section
- to choose the most inspiring option to work on

Questions could include:

- 'What idea inspires you most?'
- 'What would you like to have a go at?'
- 'What do you need to do now to move you one step towards your goal?'
- 'When are you going to start?'
- 'What might you gain from doing this?'
- 'What might you lose from doing this?'

Realisation and Review

Aim:

- to make sense of what has been realised in the session
- to confirm what has been decided and gain commitment

Questions could include:

- 'What do you feel you have learned (about yourself) from this session?'
- 'How will that help you in the future?'
- 'What are you actually committing to do?'
- 'What support do you want from me?'

It is important that the Mentee summarises their action plan, not you. This encourages ownership and commitment. The energy in their voice can help you to judge their level of commitment. If you do not hear a certain excitement and eagerness to get started, then more work is needed to check that the chosen goal/target is in alignment with their values and that any limiting beliefs have been positively dealt with.

Regular reviews throughout the mentoring period are important to monitor and celebrate progress.

CHAPTER FOUR

CHALLENGE WHEN NECESSARY

What young people believe about themselves, others and their situation impacts massively on how they behave, interpret things and ultimately perform.

One dictionary definition of a belief is "a principle or idea, accepted as true, especially without proof." This concept of accepting something as true, whether it is true or not, is key to the understanding of the impact of both empowering and limiting beliefs on a young person's performance.

There are three ways in which beliefs can affect behaviour. They can:

- Stop you from doing things if you think you cannot do them
- Make you fail at things if you believe you cannot do them
- Give you the confidence to do things if you believe that you can

As we have already seen, one of the key skills of mentoring is listening. When you hear a Mentee using negative self-talk, then it is important to raise their awareness so that they can choose to speak more positively and supportive to themselves. We are not there to collude with our Mentees so challenging limiting beliefs appropriately is part of our role. Again, the question here is 'Do you need to be liked or do you want to be respected?'

Dealing with limiting beliefs
Once a negative, limiting belief has been recognised and acknowledged by a Mentee, then with permission as the Mentor, you can:

1. Challenge it
'I always mess up' can be challenged in several ways.

Using the one word question 'always?' can challenge a Mentee to see that they are generalising.

'When didn't you mess up?' can start a Mentee looking for positive evidence with which to dismantle the unhelpful belief.

A simple but effective question can be *'how does it serve you to believe this about yourself?'*

The obvious answer is that it doesn't. But this simple realisation can start a Mentee thinking more positively about themselves and looking for ways to encourage themselves more.

Humour can be helpful, if appropriate here, as it can support a young person to resist being hard on themselves.

2. Encourage your Mentee to create a positive, empowering belief

A question such as *'What can you choose to say/believe that is more supportive of you?'* can quickly encourage your Mentee to start formulating a simple phrase or sentence that they can use to change a limiting belief.

It is important at this stage to check that the new belief is believable! Going from hopeless to fantastic in one stage can for some people be beyond belief. No amount of affirmation will overcome an exaggerated new belief. This stage is akin to the Exploration section of the **MENTOR** model and not designed to be limiting at all, just realistic.

Sometimes, simple is best – *'I can do this'* is great as it covers so many issues that people can limit themselves about. A new belief does not have to be complicated. What is important here is that the new belief and the way it is worded comes from the young person and that it is meaningful to them.

3. Support your Mentee as they search for positive evidence to reinforce this new belief.

It is vital at this point that all other interested parties such as their teachers, adult carers etc. are aware of what the young person is looking to achieve, so that they can also encourage and support them.

When someone is used to recognising negative evidence to support a negative belief, it can sometimes take time to recognise different, positive evidence. New behaviour often does not get transferred back into the classroom effectively because the first attempt at doing something new does not always work. Young people then simply revert to how they were in the past. Peer pressure has an enormous influence here.

So, too, with seeking different evidence to support a different belief. Hence the power of mentoring. As a young person tries to identify different evidence, regular mentoring sessions can support their efforts because the Mentor is only listening for what did work and not for what did not work. This is powerful reinforcement in a crucial period of change as the new belief becomes embedded.

An outcome to be aware of is that a young person may appear low or even sad initially during this process of change. Why is this? Even though a Mentee has chosen to change an unsupportive belief about themselves, this original belief was known and familiar (an old friend even!). A sense of loss can occur that again benefits from the positive reinforcement that mentoring can offer.

Shaping a new belief

The positive reinforcement that mentoring can offer in the crucial early stages of change include:

1. Positive outcome

In any change process, young people tend to succeed only if the benefits are likely to outweigh the costs. By encouraging a Mentee to focus on the benefits and positive outcomes of this new belief, a Mentor can offer valuable support to the embedding of a new belief.

The benefits that can be considered may also extend beyond the Mentee to others. Exploring this if appropriate can also enhance the motivation that your Mentee needs to succeed in changing a belief.

2. Positive actions

Changing a belief requires changing a habit or pattern.

Gaining commitment from a young person to take a first step in line with the new belief ensures that the belief becomes real and the habit or pattern is also going to change.

3. Positive reinforcement

Positive reinforcement using an affirmation can be very helpful. This can be as simple as repeating the new belief that was formulated in the 'dealing with a limiting belief' stage.

What is key here is that an affirmation is:

- Personal – I have confidence in myself
- Positive – I can manage my anger
- In the present tense – I can do this

Continual repetition can influence the unconscious mind and support the altering of limiting beliefs.

Affirmations can support actions and actions support affirmations.

4. Positive acknowledgement

Supporting a young person to focus on what is working and not what is not working during this phase is essential. Encouraging a Mentee to acknowledge themselves each time positive evidence is recognised, is also a powerful way to take this change one step at a time. Some Mentees may wish to record their achievements in some way.

Changing a belief can take time, especially if has been held over many years. Tolerance and patience are qualities that a Mentor can encourage a Mentee to show of themselves.

In summary, the role of a Mentor is:

- **B**uilding an awareness – some beliefs are
- **E**mpowering, others are
- **L**imiting. Mentoring
- **I**nvites change. This leads to
- **E**liciting a new, positive belief.
- **F**inding new, positive evidence to support it is crucial to
- **S**ustaining this new belief

If a young person needs to be challenged regarding their attitude/ behaviour then a useful model to remember is **REPS**. This is a non-combative approach to challenging.

RESPECT – Respect that this is the Mentee's map of the world

EMPATHISE – Facing up to a deeply held belief can be very uncomfortable for the Mentee – remain empathetic

PRESERVE – Always preserve rapport. Challenge softly at first.

STATE – Continue to state the positives to maintain self-esteem

The following diagram is also a reminder of how to engage a young person when needing to discuss their behaviour. They are in control of their behaviour and by having a dialogue as represented by this diagram, it ensures that they do not perceive the conversation as a direct attack on them as a person. This preserves their self-esteem whilst still inviting them to own their behaviour.

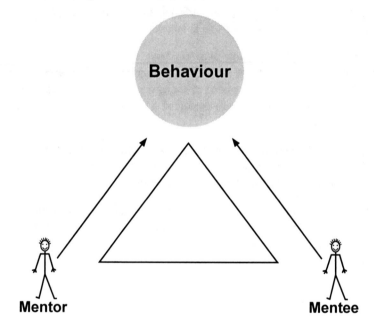

Managing Difficult Emotions

Although as Mentors we are not in the business of helping our Mentees to heal past hurts and move out of overwhelming distress, there are times when, however emotionally healthy they are, they will experience emotions, which are upsetting, overwhelming or simply unwelcome. Knowing how to deal with these feelings is invaluable in self-management.

Having recognised what a young person is feeling, and acknowledged its validity, how do they then go on to manage the emotions appropriately?

They need to know how to express negative emotions in a harmless and productive way or to postpone expressing them until a better time. As well as learning to assert positive feelings such as hope, love and joy.

What constitutes "difficult emotion"? The expression of certain emotions is acceptable in society, for instance: mild pleasure, displeasure and irritation, but it seems to be the perceived "negative emotions" which are most frowned upon and therefore most likely to be experienced as distressing or out of control.

If a young person complicates the basic feeling by "beating themselves up" emotionally for feeling it, they can enter a descending negative spiral of emotion which can easily begin to feel out of their control.

The messages from society like "big boys don't cry", "pull yourself together", and even "it'll all end in tears" as a response to "excessive" mirth, suggest that all expression of strong emotion is unacceptable. As a result, most of us have been prevented from dealing with them in an effective way.

Feelings are real, but they are not always reality, meaning that it is a young person's beliefs about their situation which inform the feelings they have about it, as much as the actual situation.

Many different factors can affect an emotional response to any situation, including: previous experience, health, energy levels, and especially the beliefs held about themselves and the world around them, and the self-talk resulting from those beliefs.

A start to coping with some of these difficult emotions is to examine what beliefs are reflected by the feelings they experience.

The ABC model used in Cognitive Behavioural Therapy can be useful in deconstructing the process:

A = the activating event (e.g. a telling off by an authority figure)

B = underlying beliefs (e.g. 'why is it always me', 'you're picking on me')

C = emotional and behavioural consequences (e.g. resentment, anger)

The young person has connected the telling off with being victimised. So a question to pose could be 'What is the evidence that you are being victimised?'

As a result of questioning and reasoning, the aim is to arrive at a realisation with your Mentee of:

- *What are the consequences of my behaviour?*
- *I need to own my own behaviour.*

In the event that your Mentee is overcome by emotion of any kind, it is your ability as a Mentor to respond appropriately which is crucial. The expression of emotion, however "negative" is normal and healthy, and not to be feared or avoided within the mentoring session.

Most often, after a short episode of crying, raging or whatever, the expression of emotion allows the Mentee to move forward and start to look at what is going on, and to design an effective way forward. It may also lead to a different, more positive way of behaving.

In the situation where a Mentee is completely overwhelmed by their feelings and unable to return to the focus of the session, it would be more appropriate to bring the session to an end and arrange to speak at another time to discuss what they need, to deal with the situation.

Feelings of shame, guilt and envy, when they are not completely disabling to a Mentee, can be dealt with very effectively by examining the underlying limiting beliefs and challenging them.

If young people are encouraged to take responsibility for their feelings, rather than blaming other people or circumstances; recognising that it is their own reaction to events which produces the feelings, they are in a much stronger position to deal with them effectively. This is true empowerment as their emotions are no longer at the mercy of other people.

Being aware of the boundaries of mentoring are essential. Engaging regularly with a Supervisor is an important part of the professionalism of being a Mentor. A Supervisor is there to support you and provide you with ongoing guidance.

Finally, let's look at Transactional Analysis and how this understanding can support both you and your Mentee when in a challenging exchange.

Transactional Analysis (TA)

Transactional Analysis (TA) is a system of thought, therapy and education originally conceived by Eric Berne in the 1950's, and further developed by others since his death in 1970. Berne's original theory of personality sees each of us operating at any one time in one of three ego states, Parent, Adult or Child. These states are mostly independent of our actual age and role in life and are collections of all we have absorbed from significant people in our lives – parents, grandparents, older siblings, teachers, religious leaders, and so on.

William Stewart in his book 'Building Self-Esteem' describes the characteristics of these three states very effectively.

The **Parent** ego state has two functions: the Critical Parent and the Nurturing Parent.

The Critical Parent:
- Equates to conscience
- Controls behaviour; sets limits; administers discipline, prescriptions, sanctions, values, instructions, injunctions, restrictions, criticism, rules and regulations; finds fault; judges
- Is power orientated

The Nurturing Parent:
- Provides warmth, support, encouragement, love, caring
- Gives advice, guides, protects, teaches how to, keeps traditions
- Is in all relationships in which we felt warmth and acceptance, not being judged
- Is caring orientated

The **Adult** ego state functions as follows:
- Gathers, stores and processes information, including memories and feelings
- Is reality-orientated: decides what is, not what should be
- Is objective; decides what fits, where and what is most useful
- Is concerned with all the processes that help the person develop well-being
- Is analytical, rational and non-judgmental
- Is a collection of all the people who have responded to us as equals, reasoned with us, shown wisdom, not patronised us
- Is rationality orientated

The **Child** ego state has two functions: The Free or Natural Child and the Adapted Child.

The Free or Natural Child:
- Is concerned with being creative, loving, curious, carefree, spontaneous, intuitive, perceptive, and with having fun
- Is adventurous, trusting, joyful
- Is the spontaneous, eager and playful part of the personality
- Is the most valuable part of the personality (Berne)
- Is creativity orientated

People whose natural child is too dominant generally lack self-control.

The Adapted Child:
- Is angry, rebellious, frightened and conforming
- Fights authority, challenges accepted wisdom and struggles for autonomy
- Is compliant and prone to sulking
- Is manipulative, protesting, submissive, placating, attention-seeking
- Is approval orientated

Berne's unit of communication is the "transaction", which occurs between individuals, each operating from one of the three ego-states. The success of each transaction depends on the complementary nature of the response, e.g, if the initial communication (transactional stimulus) is Parent to Child, the complementary response would be from Child to Parent.

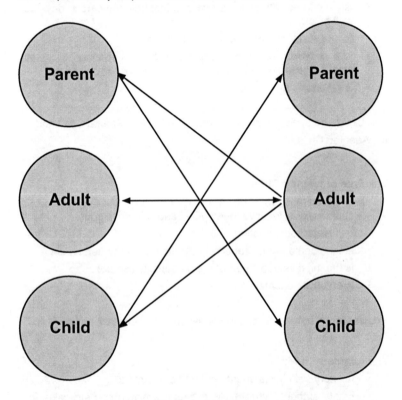

So if a Mentor were to adopt a frowning, finger-pointing, judgmental stance towards their Mentee, using words such as, 'you must, you have to', it would not be surprising if the Mentee shouted back, 'shan't, stamped their feet and slammed the door as they left!

Berne describes a basic unit of recognition, which he calls a "stroke". This can be positive (eg a compliment, a hug etc) or negative (e.g. a criticism). Without strokes we cannot survive, so that in the absence of positive strokes, a young person will seek negative ones, whether physical, verbal or non-verbal.

Berne also described "life positions" as the basic beliefs we hold about ourselves and others, based on our early experience. The two possibilities for one individual are "OK" or "not OK", so that the belief I may hold about myself relative to the rest of the world may be:

- "I'm OK, you're OK"
- "I'm OK, you're not OK"
- "I'm not OK, you're OK
- "I'm not OK, you're not OK.

The healthy and well-functioning position is "I'm OK, you're OK.

Berne's most famous book, 'Games People Play', explores the relationship patterns we repeat endlessly, which he calls "games". He gave these games witty, apposite names like

- "Let's you and him fight"
- "See what you made me do"
- "If it weren't for you" and the very familiar
- "Why don't you – yes but"

which make the process easy to spot in our own behaviour and others.

This is only a very brief description of some of the most important theories of TA, some of which may be familiar to many people, especially the "Critical Parent" and "Free Child" which have passed into common parlance.

As a Mentor you may find it useful to assess what ego state and life positions you and your Mentee are in. The mentoring relationship ideally operates in Adult:Adult mode. If a flavour of "Parent" or "Child" appears in the interaction, it would be useful to recognise that and think about what is happening. When mentoring, it is important that the Mentee takes responsibility for their actions and then the communication will remain mostly in healthy Adult:Adult.

CHAPTER FIVE

ENCOURAGING INDEPENDENCE

Encouraging independence is all about encouraging young people to truly understand themselves and to be comfortable with who they are. We have dealt with beliefs and how to encourage young people to hold positive, affirming beliefs about themselves. Understanding their values is another important part of this process.

Values

Values are "our blueprint for a fulfilled life. They are our internal compass and whether we are aware of it or not, they impact our behaviours, reactions to events and the decisions we make."

Hyrum Smith, quoted above, writes in his book 'What Matters Most' that values are "what we believe to be of the highest priority and of the greatest importance in our lives."

When our values are being acknowledged, life is good – we feel valued, respected, we feel good about ourselves and our place in the world, we're motivated, and our behaviour reflects that motivation. This is particularly visible with young people.

When conflict arises in a school situation, you may hear young people making comments such as, 'you're dissing me', ' don't bother', 'whatever.'

These are examples of values being trampled on, which leads to stress and conflict, potentially negative behaviour and attitude. Personal values are our motivators, the reason we do what we do, and we are who we are.

Encouraging young people to know their values encourages them to live their lives in alignment with these values.

Many schools have values and mission statements and these are a 'blueprint' for how they operate; their attitude towards their students. Honouring these values and engaging students with these values produces outstanding schools.

You can help a young person to understand what their values are by asking questions such as:

- *What do you value in a friend?*
- *What does it mean to be a good friend?*
- *What do I value about my family?*

When a young person is frustrated or angry, it is often because a core value is being dishonoured.

Helping them to work out which one can start a positive discussion about what to do to change the situation.

- *What makes you angry?*
- *What makes you sad?*

Eliciting core values can be a very powerful way to start a mentoring relationship. Not only do we get a chance to better understand the Mentee, it helps us to monitor the relationship between a Mentee's values, beliefs and goals/targets. When they are in alignment, it is an unstoppable combination.

A final thought here. Young people know their rights these days but some are not always so sure of their responsibilities. Encouraging them to honour society's core values (e.g. honesty, integrity, respect, punctuality, loyalty), both in and out of school is a fundamental step in becoming an independent member of society. As a Mentor, you can be a powerful role model.

Encouraging independence can also be achieved by being aware of when a Mentee is becoming dependent.

Having an understanding of transference and counter-transference may be useful here.

Unconscious processes like transference and counter-transference can be powerful because they are initially hidden. They can produce surprising and potentially unwanted elements into the relationship and you need to be aware of these and be able to detect them and deal with them to everyone's benefit if they occur.

Transference/Counter Transference

Transference can occur when:

- A Mentee unconsciously projects onto a Mentor qualities or traits belonging to a significant other person in their life. This can often be a parent figure, or a person in authority in some way, e.g. a teacher, and is often someone from the past.

Counter-transference can occur when:

- A Mentor feels tempted to respond to the Mentee in an authoritarian way.

An example of these two scenarios might be for example, that the Mentee might have a disrespect of authority and transfer these feelings to the Mentor. If the Mentor has in turn the unconscious need to be autocratic, this counter-transference can result in conflict and a lack of growth on the part of the Mentee.

Examples of transference and counter-transference may also be present in the way the Mentee interacts with their friends or colleagues, and the Mentor will need to be aware of this.

If you have any concern that transference may have entered into your relationship, then going through the following exercise may prove useful.

'Who am I?' Exercise

Mentor: "Who do I remind you of?" (repeats this gently until Mentee identifies someone)

Mentee: You remind me of 'x'

Mentor: In what ways do I remind you of 'x'?

Mentee: Finds as many ways as possible, including subtle clues like facial expression, tonalities in voice etc. Continue to prompt by asking 'how else?'

Mentor: What would you like to say to 'x'?

Mentee: says whatever is left unsaid to 'x', as though you were that person. You need to stay centred and remember that you are not 'x', and that nothing said by your Mentee actually relates to you. Putting aside any strong reaction to be dealt with after the changeover works best.

Mentor: Is there anything else you would like to say to 'x'? (repeats until Mentee has nothing left to say to 'x'

Mentor: In what ways am I different from 'x'? ...."how else?" (repeat until Mentee is unable to think of any further differences)

Mentor: Who am I?

If Mentee is unable to say "You are (your name)", without hesitation, return to unfinished business to check whether anything is left unsaid, then ask Mentee to find more differences, however subtle, between x and yourself until he is able to say unequivocally "you are (your name)".

In essence, the mentoring relationship, like all other relationships, is affected by the level of emotional intelligence of those that are involved. The Mentor can help the relationship by being aware of these factors, and taking responsibility for their own development. However, mentoring is not counselling or psychotherapy, and the Mentor needs to be very careful when faced with any of the situations, such as those above, that may be best helped or served by a Counsellor. Supporting a Mentee to take responsibility for their own emotional well-being with someone qualified to help in this way is the best support that a Mentor can give in this situation.

CHAPTER SIX

EVALUATE PROGRESS

You are probably familiar with SMART as a valuable model that supports goal setting and it also provides a useful tool for evaluating progress.

SMART
Your Mentee will have a greater chance of achieving their goals if they are aligned to the **SMART** model.

Specific
The goal must comprise a positive statement that identifies a specific outcome. Encourage your Mentee to be very specific about the goal they want to achieve. Bring the goal to life with sensory information. What will they see, hear and feel when this goal has been achieved?

Chunk down a large goal to several smaller ones if necessary. This makes it easy to evaluate progress and make appropriate changes if necessary.

Measurable
What isn't measured isn't managed. Measures must be in place in order to quantify success and to evaluate progress along the way. Work with your Mentee to put measures in place that are meaningful to them and appropriate to the end goal. Then you can encourage your Mentee to acknowledge themselves every step of the way. Some young people only have the experience of measuring failure. It can be quite a challenge for them to start recognising small successes and accepting them.

Appealing
What level of buy-in is there to this goal? Both you and your Mentee must honestly agree that this is the right way forward. If it is not appealing, it won't happen!

Realistic
The reality check that the SMART model offers will influence motivation.

Feelings of frustration may occur if goals are too high and unrealistic. Equally, if a goal is not sufficiently challenging, a young person may become de-motivated by the lack of challenge. Help your Mentee to set goals that are challenging yet not impossible. If they have a belief that they cannot achieve, then they may set themselves unrealistic goals unconsciously, simply to concur with their negative belief about themselves. Time to check out their beliefs!

Timed

Time limits are crucial to evaluating progress and keeping the Mentee on track and on target. This also provides an important opportunity to recognise every achievement along the way, however small. Setting a time limit also avoids procrastination. Be aware that young people react in different ways to pressure – some are motivated by deadlines whilst others will feel under pressure to achieve and this will have a negative influence on their motivation.

Remember capturing agreed goals/targets in a written format is important; your Mentee is more likely to achieve a goal that is written down than one that is not.

SUMMARY

DELIVER RESULTS!

In this book we have offered you our experience and some techniques we have used over the years when working with young people. We believe passionately in every young person's ability to achieve. Working with young people is the most rewarding work ever.

In choosing to mentor young people, we trust that we have also inspired you to **SUCCEED**:

Support you Mentee

Understand your Mentee

Create a learning environment

Encourage independence

Evaluate progress

Deliver results!

All that is left is to celebrate!

BIBLIOGRAPHY AND FURTHER READING

Grant, A. Greene, J. 2001. *It's your Life – what are you going to do with it? Coach yourself.*
Pearson Education Ltd. London.

Harris, T. 1995. *I'm OK – You're OK.* Arrow Books. London.

Kline, N. 2001. *Time to Think.* Ward Lock. London.

Miller, A. 2002. *Mentoring Students and Young People: A handbook of effective practice.* Routledge. London

Neenan, M., Dryden, W. 2002. *Life Coaching – a Cognitive-Behavioural Approach.* Brunner-Routledge. Hove.

Richardson, P. 2004. *Life Coach – Become the person you've always wanted to be.* Hamlyn. London

Smith, H.W. 2000. *What Matters Most.* Simon & Schuster. London.

Stewart, W. 1998. *Building Self Esteem.* How To Books. Oxford.

Whitmore, J. 2002. *Coaching For Performance.* Nicholas Brealey. London.

Williams, N. 1999. *The Work We Were Born To Do.* Element. Dorset.

LOOK OUT FOR MORE IN THIS SERIES:

To be published in 2012:

'Peer and Group Mentoring – Releasing the Potential in Young People'

Pam Richardson

Peer mentoring:
- Active Listening
- Effective questioning skills
- Developing TRUST
- Communicating confidently
- Showing respect and understanding
- Avoid making judgements.
- Managing yours and other people's feelings positively.
- Being organised.

Group   Mentoring:
- All of the above
- Running an action learning set

'Supervision – Professionalism in Practice'
Pam Richardson and John Richardson

Philosophy of Supervision
- The concept of supervision in a coaching/mentoring context
- Benefits of Supervision
- The role/responsibilities of the supervisor
- The qualities/skills/attributes of a supervisor

The Supervision Process
- Models of how to approach supervision sessions
- The Mechanics/dynamics of supervision
- Dynamics of personal supervision

The Supervisor/Supervisee Relationship
- Understanding/recognising supervisee's needs
- Understanding of learning/communication styles
- Establishing/maintaining/developing the relationship
- Formulating the supervision agreement

The Supervisor's Toolkit
- Support systems in maintaining competence/efficiency
- Systems for assessing performance constructively
- Models for evaluating & giving/receiving feedback

Ethics of Supervision

ABOUT THE AUTHORS

Pam Richardson is an internationally acclaimed Coach/Mentor, Educator and Author. Formerly Principal of Coaching and Mentoring International, she now brings her wealth of knowledge and experience to her work as a Coaching and Mentoring Partner with Intuition Discovery and Development Ltd. Her passionate belief in the unlimited potential of young people to achieve has inspired this book, which she has written with her husband, John. Together they are spearheading the Mentor training on the Military 2 Mentor programme, which they describe as the most exciting initiative they have had the privilege to be involved with.

John Richardson has been inspiring young people to achieve for over forty years. He continues to explore his passion for helping to release the potential he believes we all possess as a Coaching and Mentoring Partner with Intuition Discovery and Development Ltd. Formerly as Head of Mentoring and Supervision at Coaching and Mentoring International, John developed a range of programmes to train mentors and supervisors to the highest standards. He has now combined his extensive knowledge and experience with Pam's to produce an inspiring book to support the mentoring of young people in schools.

Lightning Source UK Ltd.
Milton Keynes UK
UKOW040614240512

193171UK00001B/1/P